# THE ULTIMATE GUIDE TO MOVING YOUR COMPANY REMOTE

JEFF ROBBINS

**DISCLAIMER**

The information in this book is based on the author's knowledge, experience and opinions. The methods described in this book are not intended to be a definitive set of instructions. You may discover other methods and materials to accomplish the same end result. Your results may differ.

There are no representations or warranties, express or implied, about the completeness, accuracy, or reliability of the information, products, services, or related materials contained in this book. The information is provided "as is," to be used at your own risk.

## Dedication

Teresa McGee was a coach at By Referral Only. At the time of our transition to 100% remote, she was 67 years old, and had worked for at By Referral Only for 18 years, our longest tenured employee aside from the founder. She handled the transition with grace and positivity, even though being in the office with her team was all that she had known for 18 years. Soon after our transition, she developed terminal cancer. She was able to work a minimal schedule for a few years while battling this terrible disease, which we were both thankful for. We lost her in 2017. I love and miss her spirit and love.

# TABLE OF CONTENTS

# FOREWORD

My name is Joe Stumpf, and in 1986, I founded By Referral Only, one of the country's largest and now oldest) business and life coaching companies. We are privileged to work with some of the most successful entrepreneurs and businesspeople every day. And while I've been dedicated to growing this business for over 30 years, we wouldn't be here without the hard work, foresight, and passion of Jeff Robbins.

I've known Jeff since 2012 when he joined the team to run operations. We were in the early stages of transitioning our company from a live seminar company to an entirely virtual company doing everything through the internet. When he joined us, we were struggling under the guidance of the current CEO, who had little experience in this new world. Jeff came to me and expressed his concerns. He shared his love for the company and our mission, and he was watching it implode. Jeff rarely comes to me with a problem if he doesn't have a solution, so together we decided to make a change.

We hired a new CEO, a person we both knew well. Together, we recruited him to be the new CEO because he had the internet marketing expertise we needed. We combined Jeff's experience running a direct sales subscription business with our new CEO's marketing expertise, which made the transition a huge success. But equally important, Jeff had the foresight to see that our future success was through converting By Referral Only to an entirely virtual company.

Under his leadership, he successfully closed our 10,000-square-foot, $50,000-fixed-overhead building in Carlsbad, California. Jeff made us a 100% remote virtual company with dozens of employees working in multiple states and did it seamlessly.

A few years later, Jeff came to me again and expressed his concerns that the culture was losing its heart. It had shifted to too much promise, not enough delivery. It had become a pure "sell them whatever you can" culture. By this time, I had come to know Jeff as a brilliant, kind, compassionate, loving man who everyone in the company deeply respected. So, in 2016, I asked Jeff to take over the role of CEO.

Then, in 2020, I had an awakening; it was time for me to shift my attention to my legacy work. Having achieved business success and enjoying great relationships with family and friends, I was reexamining my bigger purpose in life for the next 25 years, and I wanted to finish strong. I had seen far too many men, including my father, finish life getting weaker emotionally, mentally, spiritually, and physically, and I knew that if I didn't make it my primary purpose to get stronger as I grew older, I could easily slip down that path, too.

You see, I am well versed in how growth works. Our business coaching program guides our clients through the four phases of growth—from survival to stability, stability to success, and success to significance. In my experience, I have witnessed thousands of men and women go through these stages. Yet, the stage from success to significance seems reserved for only the few who dare to reinvent themselves after fully achieving worldly success. Making money and accumulating power and prestige is a matter of drive, determination, smart strategic direction, and being at the right place at the right time—taking advantage of the opportunities that present themselves. The more elusive stage of growth is significance because it seems to invite us into a way of being that requires a completely different awareness.

I had reached that point, and I knew it was time to make a significant change. Jeff and I met again, and I asked him to be my partner in By Referral Only. This helped me create the space to move to the next stage of my life and follow my desire to make a more significant contribution in the world. Today, I've made that transition, and the only way I could have done it was with the support and love of Jeff Robbins.

Because of Jeff, I was able to shift from living a life of success to living a life of significance, and By Referral Only has transformed into a successful marketing agency. He had a big vision to be the company that gets the work DONE for our clients. In this book, you get to see how strategic and methodical he is in his approach to going remote. What you don't see, however, is his amazing ability to create a loving, collaborative, peer-to-peer, accountably culture, so let me fill you in. As a leader, this is who Jeff Robbins is:

- He is encouraging, making people want to be around him all the time.
- He makes people feel good.
- He communicates clearly and often.
- He helps people overcome difficulties.
- He teaches people how to master disciplining themselves.
- He always finds the positive, no matter what happens.
- He measures his impact by how the people he leads grow as people.
- He helps people become healthier.
- He helps people become wiser.
- He helps people become more autonomous.
- He helps people become leaders.

In my experience, his greatest strength is his ability to give clarity to purpose and do it with love, respect, and kindness.

Enjoy this journey, and know Jeff is the perfect guide to lead you to work remotely and go from survival to stability, stability to success, and success to significance.

**Joe Stumpf**
PrivateWork.com
Forestville California
May 2022

# INTRODUCTION

When the COVID-19 pandemic hit in 2020, this book was in its final stages of drafting. Across the world, businesses and families were forced into working and schooling from home. Many scrambled in their attempt to manage life in a virtual way. Thankfully, my team was already settled and prepared, with years of remote working experience already under our belts. Our company, By Referral Only, after 24 years in business, had officially made the transition to full-time remote working in 2015.

Still, adjusting to business after COVID-19 wasn't easy. Our company suffered a 10 percent drop in revenue because we could no longer hold the live events we'd scheduled for 2020, but this was a far cry from the losses that other companies experienced that year. Our team was fine—more than fine, actually. We did so well that we decided to refocus our efforts and teach our clients the skills and strategies we'd learned and implemented during our transition to remote working.

Since the start of the pandemic, we've helped thousands of real estate agents and lenders in the U.S. and Canada find their way in the new remote-work environment. We assisted them as they learned how to use Zoom and other technologies to stay in touch with their sphere of influence during an unprecedented time. Those who charged forward and embraced the changes (versus hiding from them) had the best year ever!

It's been more than two years now since the pandemic surfaced. Life in the U.S. is slowly returning to normal, but many companies are still trying to decide what to do with their workforce. I see possible three options:

1.  They can stay virtual and keep their workforce working remotely. With their feet now on the ground, they will build on what they've learned and continue to improve it.
2.  They can return everyone to the office and go back to business as it was before. (Many can't wait to do this!)
3.  They can implement a hybrid format where there are days at home and other days in the office, or where certain teams stay remote and some return to the physical office.

The businesses I've spoken with are struggling with these decisions. They want to please everyone, including their shareholders—but that just isn't possible!

The reality is, pandemic or not, remote working is the way of the future—it didn't just start with the pandemic. In fact, data from Global Workplace Analytics indicated that telecommuting had already grown an estimated 103 percent between 2005 and 2014.[1] It was also predicted that 2020 would be a tipping point for remote work; analysts expected at least half of the workforce to work from home at least part of the time by then.[2] Their projections were far exceeded during the COVID-19 outbreak.

In a post-pandemic remote work study from Global Workplace Analytics, 97 percent of surveyed individuals stated they were working from home.[3] For more than half (67 percent) of the respondents, it was a new experience. While their introduction to the virtual work environment had been less than desirable, only six percent said they never wanted to work from home again. The rest were highly supportive of remote working, with 82 percent of U.S. office employees saying they preferred to keep working from home, at least part of the time. Most favored the "hybrid model," which would have them working from both their home and the office.

---

1 "Big News: Telecommuting Grew 103% in Last 10 Years" by Jessica Howington, Flexjobs, https://www.flexjobs.com/blog/post/big-news-telecommuting-grew-103-last-10-years/

2 "Why the Future of Work Is Remote" by Jennifer Parris, Remote.co, September 8, 2015, https://remote.co/why-the-future-of-work-is-remote/

3 "Survey Reveals 76% of Global Office Workers Want to Continue Working from Home post-COVID-19" by Anita Kamouri, Ph.D. and Kate Lister, Global Workplace Analytics, June 2, 2020, https://globalworkplaceanalytics.com/brags/news-releases

With statistics like these, businesses should at least consider the benefits of working (or staying) remote. Perhaps the most obvious and notable is the amount of money that companies could save—an estimated $11,000 per employee each year and as much as $500 billion a year on other expenses such as electricity, employee turnover, absenteeism, and real estate.[4] Global Workplace Analytics also determined that workplace distractions were less frequent for remote employees than those working in the office (43 minutes of "wasted time" for remote employees versus 78 minutes in-office staff).

The benefits of remote work also extend beyond the company's bottom line. Employees themselves can save between $2,000 and $7,000 on food and travel expenses each year. Global greenhouse emissions could be decreased by an estimated 54 million tons annually, and the world could save as much as 640 million barrels of oil. The number of traffic accidents would undoubtedly decrease as well—by as many as 90,000 crashes per year, according to estimates.

Unfortunately, through your experience reacting to the stay-at-home orders during the pandemic, you may have already discovered that turning a business remote isn't quite as simple as it sounds. Once the decision is made to go full-time virtual, you may have valuable employees who are resistant to the change. For a while following the transition, turnover rates may increase because some

---

4 "Big News: Telecommuting Grew 103% in Last 10 Years" by Jessica Howington, Flexjobs, https://www.flexjobs.com/blog/post/big-news-telecommuting-grew-103-last-10-years/

employees are either unwilling or incapable of working remotely. Difficulties finding the "right" technology can further compound the stress of employees and management alike. Companies must also tackle logistical hurdles and keep their employees connected and communicating while working from home, which may mean your team spans cities and even states. Managers must also learn how to foster a culture of trust and lean into a different way of leading; many of the supervisory tactics and practices used for offices don't convert to the virtual workspace.

In my career, I've spent more than 20 years optimizing the operations and logistics of companies. I've tackled upsizing, downsizing, and everything between. I've struggled with the restrictions of a physical office in both my personal and professional life. Then, in 2015, everything changed. The company I work for started to entertain the idea of a virtual office. From the start, I recognized remote working as the future of the workforce. I was excited to take on the challenge.

The executive management team addressed what going virtual would mean for our bottom line, employee well-being, and customer satisfaction. After careful consideration, we opted to forgo a gradual transition and, instead, embraced going completely virtual as soon as reasonably possible. In my role as operations manager for our company, I spent the greater part of the following year researching, planning, and preparing our team for the transition.

There were many doubts about whether we could transition without a loss of productivity and profit, but the office lease was ending, and we had no plan for a new office. There was no backup plan and there was no turning back. I led the charge to a 100 percent virtual office. We closed the physical office space and sent each employee home with the technology they would need to provide a seamless experience for our customers.

Fast-forward to today, my company has seen increased profitability and productivity. My team is still 100 percent remote. No one has quit, and morale is at an all-time high. The hiring process is different, but the personnel pool is larger, and the benefit of working remotely is HUGE to prospective employees. The best part of all? In addition to the fact that we've been able to pay these benefits forward to our clients during the pandemic, they never experienced a hitch in any of our operations or customer service. Our clients never even knew.

When we first decided to move the company remote, I couldn't find any resources to guide me through the process. This book aims to fill that gap. It contains everything we've learned through the process of moving 100 percent remote, and it can serve as a blueprint to help you navigate through the relatively unchartered territory of a virtual office. No matter your company's location or industry, it will help you understand what goes into such a significant move. However, this material is specifically geared toward guiding a private local or regional company with less than a handful of locations in a non-retail industry. In other words, the book will deliver the most value to those companies that have the capacity to take their entire workforce virtual without feeling tied to some type of onsite functionality. (If you believe your company to fall outside of that scope, the material is still applicable but needs to be calibrated for your size, location, or industry needs.)

The person reading this book and implementing the strategies will most likely be a facilities manager, operations manager, or project manager; it should be someone who knows the nuts and bolts of what you'll need to do to pull off the transition.

Once you've decided to move forward to a virtual workplace, this field-tested guide provides you with the steps and information you need to ensure a smoother transition, including what I wish I had known before I started.

As time goes on, this new way of working will continue to evolve and improve. Technology and best practices will change to meet the growing demand. A virtual workforce goes beyond technology implementation, however; it's also about finding a new way of leading and managing people by creating a culture of trust. It is about getting the work done, which can be quite a challenge when you no longer have the benefit of walking down the hallway and collaborating with your peers, connecting with your direct reports, or running something by your manager. There aren't any opportunities for quick drop-ins when you need the answer to a question. The team is forced to be more diligent, efficient, and thorough.

I hope this book brings some foundational insight and guidance to help propel your company forward. Change is difficult for most people, but it's also necessary (and often beneficial). And, in some cases, change can be the catalyst that launches you into success. Such is often the case for those who fully embrace the virtual workspace.

From one business professional to another, I encourage you to get in early and ride the wave versus getting crushed by it! And please consider me as a resource as you go on this journey. I'm available to answer questions and give relevant advice based on what I'm seeing as it relates to the current environment.

# CHAPTER 1

# GETTING READY TO GO REMOTE

I can't think of a single business that doesn't have at least some elements that could be virtual.  Many corporations have chosen to be 100 percent in-person, simply because the leadership of the company "always did it this way" and achieved certain levels of success. Will these companies be able to attract and retain talent if they only operate "the old way"?

The pandemic gave millions of people the experience of working remotely. Some loved it. Some hated it. Either way, most will simply move on if they are unhappy with the decisions their company made, especially if they can find someone willing to offer them better pay or more perks (i.e., working virtually at least part of the time). Once the decision of shifting to a remote office is made, a company must prepare. Hopefully, steps are taken before the best employees start moving to other companies that are more flexible and open to a flexible workplace. This book assumes you've already decided to go virtual (at least part-time) and want to learn more about HOW to make this happen in your business.

This chapter will walk you through what needs to happen to prepare your employees, management, and internal operations to go remote and help you begin to produce an outline of what specifically needs to be done as you move toward your move-out date.

## Transition Timeline

In a perfect world, your company would be 100 percent remote-capable before closing the doors on its physical location(s)—in this perfect world, your company will have taken steps to gradually ease into this transition. This means, even while still operating from the office, employees would be comfortable working from home tomorrow, without notice or preparation. The transition would be smooth, and everyone would embrace their new, virtual roles with open arms. Unfortunately, we do not live in a perfect world. Even years before an actual global pandemic made it mandatory, I practically had to *force* some of my staff members to work from home! The pandemic pushed so many other companies down this same road.

How long you need to plan ahead before the official

transition will depend on many factors, including how much must be changed before you move. If every system is physically located inside your brick-and-mortar building, you will have a bigger transition and need more time. If some of your business records and files are already stored virtually, you will have less preparation. The key is not to try to tackle everything in the 30 days before your move or you'll have a serious mess on your hands. Instead, I recommend implementing your changes gradually and in a strategic manner.

Once our company's executive management team made the official decision, I started preparing our local company of about 40 employees by dropping hints about the move around 18 months before the company's lease expired. About nine months out, I started talking with some employees directly about the transition. My earliest discussions were with HR and the department managers. I wanted to know which team members would make the transition easily and which ones would have difficulties. I knew HR's and each team manager's level of involvement would depend on many different factors, and I wanted to get them on board as early as possible.

Determining when to start making changes to the employees' daily operations should be given some serious thought. Depending on how long the team has been together, there can be interruption to some deep-rooted patterns on the social side that you'll need to consider. For example, in addition to my operational duties, I still manage the coaching division, and half of my direct team had worked in the same office together for five years or more. They were very set in their behaviors around the break-room, lunch, happy hour, and other social connections. As a result, I knew I wanted to ensure they had enough time to ease into the transition and find ways to continue their connections virtually.

To help with this, about a year before our virtual transition, I gave my employees one requirement: to work from home at least one day a month. Before long, I could separate my team into three groups: 1) those who eagerly accepted the task and couldn't wait to go fully virtual, 2) the ones who were capable but hadn't put much thought or effort into the assignment, and 3) a final group that I practically had to drag out of the office to get them involved.

Those who were capable needed some prodding, but once I pushed them a little, they began to enjoy their new virtual role. The highly resistant group required a great deal of hand holding in the beginning, but they slowly acclimated to the change. Then, about six months before our planned closure, we were forced into an unplanned remote working "test run." It turned out to be an invaluable, eye-opening experience.

Fires in Southern California were approaching our office and we had to evacuate. I sent everyone home for three or four days. The company didn't close for a minute. Skype chat blew up. Everyone learned how to efficiently interact with their team in a virtual office setting and how effective technology can be in a time of crisis.

Many other companies in our area simply closed. They

weren't able to help their customers and experienced a complete loss of productivity—and undoubtedly profits—in those few days. A fire may not have been the most ideal testing grounds, but the experience proved that we were on the right path. The steps we'd already taken meant we were well on our way... but we still had some things that needed tweaking. Our "practice run" helped reveal these issues, which is why I highly recommend (planned) week-long tests, prior to going 100 percent virtual. You don't know what you don't know, so make this a priority and deal with all the glitches before the small issues become big ones.

Here's an at-a-glance summary of our company's general roll-out timeline to help you create your own. Again, keep in mind that your timeline may vary depending upon your location, company size, industry, and current virtual status. For example, a bigger company may have much more work to do to fully transition but might decide to do a gradual transition in phases while allowing employees to work flex time (in or out of the office at their discretion) for a certain amount of months before going completely virtual. A smaller company may be able to get it all done in six months and pull the plug without much lead time to the move-out date. Do what's best for your company; this is what worked best for ours.

| Months Before Move-Out | |
|---|---|
| 18 months | Firm decision made to move to remote working environment |
| 18 months | Start dropping hints about the move |
| 12 months | Start having conversations with key management and HR staff |
| 12 months | Company-wide announcement should be made |
| 9 months | Begin executing transition plan, including technology training and asset management steps |
| 9 months | Require employees to work from home at least one day a month |
| 6 months | Implement week-long test runs |
| 2 months | Require employees to work from home one day a week |
| 1 month | Require employees to work from home 50% of the time |

## Choosing a Move-Out Date

How do you determine your final "move out" date? Normally, it'll revolve around the expiration of a building lease, but this is not always the case. The CFO will be very interested in making sure that you achieve all the savings of the remote environment possible, so their vote is usually for the end of the lease. It generally makes sense to time it this way, but other factors may influence the date of your move as well. Examples might include a technology commitment, a merger or acquisition, or the impending sale of your company's building.

Regardless of the final move date, the decisions you make today should be made with the future in mind. For example, if Bill in accounting needs a new computer now, what kind are you going to get him—a replacement for his current desktop or a new laptop? I originally thought we would all take our desktop systems home and use them, which, at the time, made sense for a larger company. I turned out to be wrong. As we found out, laptops offer a certain level of flexibility that may be needed in a work-from-home environment, which I'll talk about in a later chapter. Knowing things like this well before the move-out date will help align your daily operational decisions with the company's future virtual success.

Just don't let the process of going remote become too distracting or stressful. While it's perfectly normal to want to "get it right," the transition shouldn't negatively impact your clients or customers. In fact, the end goal should be minimal disruption to daily operations. Much of this can be achieved by giving yourself enough lead time prior to the move-out date. Again, don't wait until the last few months or weeks to squeeze it all in. Planning ahead makes your life easier and instills confidence in your employees that this will be a beneficial move for the company and them.

# Creating a Culture of Trust

Many managers use the "management by walking around" method. They chit-chat with people of interest to find out what's going on in a specific department or with a particular person and to obtain an overall impression of how things are going in their team. While this management style is common, it is extremely ineffective in remote working environments—in fact, it literally does not work unless you want to go door to door and visit your team members at home each day. And while I hope this goes without saying for most managers, it's also important to know that the fear, threats, and manipulation used by strict supervisors are useless in the virtual office (not to mention highly outdated, given what we know about leadership today).

In my experience, remote workspaces are more efficient and gratifying when you foster a culture of trust. This requires you to mindfully and intentionally show your team members that you trust them to show up, do a great job, and work well within the new virtual world. For most, this will be an organizational-level culture shift; it requires a new way of operating from top down. But, not everyone on your team will thrive. Some employees will struggle. Knowing how to better lead them might encourage a portion of the hesitant into compliance, but you will undoubtedly deal with those who are either unwilling to or incapable of performing in a remote environment. Ideally, you want to avoid bringing these people on once you've made the decision to go remote, but if you already employ these individuals, tough decisions may need to be made.

One of the best places to start shifting the culture is by trading outdated strategies for more effective leadership strategies. One example includes implementing KPIs (key performance indicators), which allow you to watch and track performance so you know productivity is improving once your team goes remote. Face-to-face interaction via video chat is another critical component in remote working spaces. We'll delve further into the importance of KPIs and video chats—and strategies for getting the most out of these virtual meetings—later in this guide. For now, we'll take a closer look at what's necessary for creating a thriving remote working environment—and again, much of this comes down to trust.

If your current office culture doesn't have trust built into it, you can't just flip a switch and make it happen. It's like a dog that's been chained up for years and only knows his circle. Oftentimes, you unchain the dog and it stays in its circle. Other times, the dog runs away. Your employees can behave like this as well—especially if you fail to incorporate trust into your culture prior to the move.

How do you create trust? An entire book is necessary to address this topic, but a good place to start is with verbalizing it. "We trust that you continue to be efficient, and to accomplish your work within the guidelines we've established. We hope that you enjoy the benefit of having no commute, having your pets near you, and having more flexibility in your schedule. As long as our metrics stay positive, we'll be able to stay in this environment, etc."

Your employees will work harder to stay in the remote environment. They'll want to prove that "this works." When my son started driving, I had to trust that he was making good decisions while out and about. What other choice did I have? Installing cameras in his car? Me riding with him everywhere? I just had to trust and have some faith that he would make the right decisions. It's no different when transitioning your team to remote; it all starts with trust.

## Get Comfortable with Technology

There could be an entire book on all the technical aspects of setting up your workforce to work remotely. I'm not smart enough (or experienced enough) to write that book! Much of it depends on the size and infrastructure of your company. What I can do is highlight some of the important aspects of what you need to be prepared to implement that can make the transition smoother for the team. After all, the best technologies in the world are useless if you don't take care of preparing and training your crew to use them.

If you are the leader of this project, make sure that all the technical areas are covered by an expert. If you don't have one on your team, go out and find one... because you can't fail at this.

Technology is a huge part of the migration and the transformation to a remote office, and with the vast array of options available, the decisions and processes leading up to full implementation can be overwhelming. Startups often have an edge because they don't have to "unbolt" old technologies and can start fresh with great tools, but even well-established companies can make a smooth transition.

Your technology strategy should depend on where your company stands with it now. When I started at By Referral Only, we had 22 servers in two separate co-hosting locations in Southern California. Realistically, the servers were about five years behind their time. As a result, our first step to going remote was to move all of our servers to the cloud.

Whether you're starting from scratch or unbolting an entire system, I predict you'll find something you can start working on TODAY. On almost a daily basis, there's a new player in the industry offering a solution to common business-related issues. Identify the different areas of your technology (workstation hardware, servers/routers/domain controllers, collaboration and communication software, and anything else proprietary to your business), then assess what technologies should stay, what needs to go, and what can be modified.

I recommend creating a spreadsheet with all these categories so that you can start the discussion. (See Appendix A for a sample list). As far as what to use for all the aspects working remotely brings onboard, we'll cover that in Chapter 2. Your mission now is to just get the conversation rolling. I can't emphasize this enough: start the discussion asap! Get your key people thinking about this. You'll want all brains on the planning part.

## What to Do with the Warehouse

Company warehouses can vary greatly in size, ranging from a small room where files, supplies, and equipment are stored to a large, dedicated building that ships hundreds or thousands of SKUs each day. In either case, I encourage you to consider doing away with your warehouse and finding another solution for your company's storage and shipping needs.

My operations background started in the warehouse, working in a third-party fulfillment center. I've had experience with both in-house and outside logistic solutions. At the last three companies I worked with, my key objective was to outsource the warehouse and distribution department.

In general, you should not be doing your shipping and distribution in-house. Moving your whole office to remote and keeping your warehouse is silly, especially when there are companies that specialize in warehouse and distribution. Their space and labor are often cheaper, and they have specialized employees in distribution. Plus, if their guy has a difficult day and ships the wrong product, it's on their dime, not yours.

Based on my experience, so much time, effort, and cost goes into running your own warehouse that outsourcing makes more sense—even if the numbers don't initially look like they will balance out in your favor. Don't believe me? There's an exercise that can help illustrate the cost of running your own warehouse.

You probably already have some of this data showing as a KPI or broken out in your financials. It's usually not as clean as you would like, and you might have to piece some areas of data together, but it should give you a rough idea on how much you could stand to save by outsourcing your shipping.

On an average month, calculate the following:

- Warehouse-related labor
- Space allocation costs
- Number of orders shipped
- Average number of line items per order
- Any special equipment rental costs
- Any other direct related warehouse expenses

Most logistics companies charge a base price per order, and then an additional price for each SKU. An example might be $2.00 per order and $1.00 per additional SKU picked. Calculate the rough math and figure out what your average cost is per order, then break it down to determine your average line-item cost. When I did this exercise at By Referral Only, we were paying five times the cost of outsourcing... and doing far more work than necessary. (See Appendix B for sample spreadsheet.)

Once the decision to move to third-party fulfillment is made, it's time to start shopping. There are vendors who specialize in small, medium, and large storage/shipping volumes. As you make your calls, know the specifics of what you're shipping each day/week/month, how many orders you receive each month (on average), how many line items per order on a monthly/annual basis, and your overall storage needs. You don't want to be the big fish in a small pond, or the small fish in a big pond, so determine your size and seek out a vendor that handles other accounts your size.

How close your business is to a major city will determine whether you can find a local third-party logistics/fulfillment vendor. I like local, if possible, because someone can go visit easily, which is nice when you are transitioning. If there aren't options close to you, consider companies in the Midwest. You might be able to shave off some of the transit time for your customers by finding a more centralized location.

Since a great deal of work goes into preparing your account to ship within their system, many third-party order fulfillment/logistics companies will require a setup fee, so plan for this expense ahead of time. It's highly likely that you'll need to optimize your order processing system, as most fulfillment centers accept orders via electronic format. Once the order is received, the vendor will print a packing slip or invoice, pick the order items, and ship the orders to your customers. Your customer service department will likely still handle customer order inquiries, so you might also need to add a feedback system that will allow your company to retrieve tracking numbers, shipping dates, and other pertinent order information from the fulfillment center.

Depending on the size of your distribution center, you might even want to consider having an employee manage the third-party warehouse full-time. Smaller warehouses could likely be handled by someone in your operations department as part of their other duties. Purchasing, inventory control, and warehouse have great synergies. This style of combined management and oversight works well with purchasing because they are delivering the goods to the warehouse and watching inventory levels as part of their regular job.

## What to Do with Business Documents

Even if you don't have a warehouse, it's likely that your company is storing office supplies and equipment (and maybe some personal items that belong to the company owner) in a back room somewhere. It's time to start thinking about where these things will go. You also may have accounting and HR-related boxes stored somewhere on your property. Most third-party warehouse companies don't want these documents or the risk of housing them. Depending on your HR rules and the specifics of your company, you may agree. There are a ton of document storage companies out there and I think they all do a fair job (Iron Mountain comes to mind as a big player).

This is a project that someone from your accounting or HR department could start working on early in the game.

Have them box, inventory, identify, correctly label, and seal those documents so they are ready to move. Your tracking spreadsheet should have an expiration date on it, based on the GAP accounting rules of storing accounting/HR documents (count on at least seven to ten years, maybe more).

Now you just need to find storage—you generally have two options here: a storage provider or a public storage space. Having your documents stored with a dedicated provider may not be as cheap as public storage, but it's the safest way to protect sensitive information. My company rented a small storage space to hold our HR documents, accounting files, and other, obscure miscellaneous items. The cost is approximately $120 per month. If a local storage space is not an option for you, you'll need to look for a company that specializes in secure document storage. Iron Mountain is one of the most well-known national providers of secure document storage. They'll come pick up your boxes and help with tracking. They normally charge per box. Search locally in your area for "secure document storage" and you'll see the other big players in your area.

I don't recommend storing items with any of your employees (unless it's something they use daily). For example, your accounting person needs checks and recent financial records. They could store these in a secure, locked cabinet in their home. (You might trust your employee, but what about their family, friends, or that long-lost pen pal staying over for the summer?) Keep in mind that if you have to terminate this person in the future, it could be very difficult to recover your important docs.

My company keeps all of its HR-related files in the cloud. Our accounting department is moving towards becoming paperless. The less we need to store with employees, the better. We rarely visit storage. Every 12 months, we visit the unit to purge any items not touched over the past year.

I made one person responsible for the storage, but there are a few backup people who also have keys, so we always have someone who can run over and get what is needed. In addition to your warehouse outsourcing project, document storage is also a project that can be started early. It's truly never too early to get someone started on this task.

# CHAPTER 2

# TECHNOLOGY IN THE NEW WORK ENVIRONMENT

Chances are, if you're in a leadership role, you've probably worked remotely at some point. Maybe it's been more sporadic (checking emails while on a trip), or perhaps it was thoughtfully planned to happen on a weekly basis. Either way, there is a distinct difference between working remotely periodically and doing so full time.

I recall picking and choosing which project to work on when I only worked from home occasionally. Now, ALL of the work must be done at home. Time must be managed efficiently, energy must be focused, and technology must be in place!

So, let's talk tech!

# Communication & Collaboration: Text-Based Tools

Generally speaking, there are two types of tools you'll want to consider using for workforce communication and collaboration when you transition to full-time remote work: text-based tools and video-based tools. These tools must take the place of all face-to-face communication that was used while your business had a physical office.

While my company was still in the office, people could simply look over a cubicle wall or walk over to someone's desk. Not a super efficient method for obtaining what they needed, but it's how the staff had interacted over their 10+ years together. We never had a reason to discourage it; they were still productive in their day, and these impromptu meetings gave them a chance to socialize and connect with their coworkers (which is still needed, even in the virtual office). As we made the transition to a remote workspace, the effectiveness of their communication became a concern.

Our company didn't incorporate an internal chat system until after I started digging into *how* they were working from home. Overall, they were about 50 percent efficient in their roles. A lot of this was because they would run into times where they didn't have something they needed to complete a certain task or project. They'd email the documents to themselves, or they'd email coworkers to get the information. Often, they were forced to shelve the project until they received a response. This was my wakeup call: email for internal company communication is DEAD!

You must embrace this going into a transition to remote working. Email cannot do the job of other more effective text-based tools that we'll talk about throughout this section. What I discovered was that without another means to communicate, the frequency of social "chat" style emails increased dramatically, which clogged up everyone's inbox and slowed down communication. Worse yet, employees were emailing files and documents back and forth because they'd forgotten a critical piece of information at the office. While this was far from a new issue, it had become hindersome in our new, virtual workspace. We needed to make some swift and immediate changes.

Our first step was to install Skype on everyone's system. I didn't think it would be the final answer for our company, but I needed a new vehicle for office chit-chat—a new method of chatting versus email versus getting up and walking over and interrupting someone. Skype was user-friendly and easy to implement, and it would work in the short term. I asked every employee to start using the chat feature in place of emails (we didn't even bother with the video features at first). It took about a month to get everybody using it. Slowly, they embraced this feature. Five years later, we transitioned to using Slack to chat and interact, but Skype definitely served as a useful learning tool in the beginning.

For your company, there may be one that works better than the other. Jump in and experiment as you go through the decision-making process prior to full transition. As you look for a system to replace email within your company, consider the other forms of communication that need to be replaced. Certainly, you'll want a system that allows for the upload and easy search of documents to minimize the back-and-forth email madness, but think of the other types of organic communication that happen within the office each day.

There are coworkers who are friends, coworkers who work closely together daily, and people who need information from someone else to do their job (typically cross-departmentally). Then there are small teams that work on collaborative projects, and departments that meet and share information regularly. Also consider the need for corporate-wide communication, like if the president or CEO needs to post a message for the entire company. Your task is to emulate what's happening inside the physical building in your virtual office. And remember, any improvement of habits that you can implement before the physical move are encouraged.

Keep in mind that your text-based collaboration tool also needs to replace the day-to-day personal interactions that workers have within the office: people talking in the break room, leaning across the cubicle to make lunch plans, or jumping out of their chair and heading across the room to ask a coworker a quick question about a current project. You may also have a bulletin board listing pertinent information, such as open enrollment for health insurance or the upcoming staff party.

If you think the remote workplace will remove the need for employee chit-chat, you're absolutely wrong. Employees need to feel connected, even (and especially) in the virtual office. Unfortunately, cohesiveness can be more difficult to achieve in a remote setting, so you'll want to choose a collaboration software that closely mimics the daily, in-office interactions of your employees.

Now that we've refined our utilization of these text-based tools over the years, our team has really embraced them. They usually visit the community chat room to say good morning, first thing, just like they did at the office. We also have a virtual break room/chat area, where "water cooler" people can talk about what they did on the weekend and show pictures of their dog, their kids, and vacations. The HR manager has a virtual bulletin board that they can use to post important information, such as the holiday schedule and OSHA notices. Our collaboration software even allows for the "liking" of comments and photos, and the adding of emojis. (I wonder where they got that idea...) This is all available through the Slack platform.

Chit-chat and socialization aren't the only forms of communication you'll be replacing. You'll also need to create teams and virtual rooms where people can share information. These "areas" will be department-based, project-based, and company-wide.

Sometimes it's better to be lucky than good. I spent about nearly 40 hours researching the best collaboration software for our business. Each platform seemed to have a specialized thing, but it seemed impossible to find one strong enough in all of the areas I needed. Then, on "decision day," I walked into my office, sat down, and noticed a new phone sitting on my desk, ready for testing. My IT guy came in and helped me get it going. We downloaded this, installed that... then I noticed a new icon on my desktop. I had no idea how long it'd been on my computer, or how it got there. My IT guy hadn't heard of the app either.

Though a bit weary and overwhelmed from all my research, I decided to click on the little "Glip" icon. That moment changed everything! Apparently, RingCentral—the company we used for our phones—had just bought Glip. The app was included in the software package we'd purchased. After about 20 minutes of browsing around in Glip, the whole office heard me scream. Anyone passing by likely saw me dancing a jig. This free app, which I hadn't even heard of, seemed like the perfect fit. Little did I know then, it would be all that, and more. For years, we used the following key features:

- **Department Meetings:** When video chat is integrated with your software program, department meetings are as simple as the click of a button. Each person on the team is called and invited. This was preferable to Skype, where you might spend a great deal of time rounding everyone up for the meeting. Integration isn't a deal breaker, but it's definitely more convenient and efficient.

- **Task Management:** Each group (or virtual room) offered the ability to assign tasks to one or more members. You could also include website links that were tracked and searchable, create events and notes, and attach files. We didn't use the events and calendar features to their full capacity, but I suppose that's because we utilized Google Calendar, (it was just too hard to compete with their features and functionality). The ability to assign tasks in Glip was also a great project management feature; I asked my team to assign me tasks when they needed me to do something. That became one of the ways to make sure I didn't drop the ball in my busy schedule.

- **Search Functionality:** A comprehensive search function should be a key feature in the collaboration system you select. If there's a popular project going on with a lot of people involved and numerous discussions, critical info may get pushed down, making it difficult to find. In Glip, important discussions were kept within their specific project room. You could also follow and read through the trail of any decisions, agreements, or disagreements made. Of course, scrolling through can become tiresome and inefficient when the data you need is old or infrequently used. Enter Glip's rock-solid search tool. It saved me countless hours!

Glip allowed us to be less dependent on Word and email, overall. And though we have since transitioned away from both Skype and Glip to Slack for text-based collaboration (Glip is no longer in existence as RingCentral acquired the app and renamed it), I still consider Glip's implementation to be our company's best decision yet. It served as a useful tool for a very long time. Slack has a lot of the same features, but as our daily work evolved, integrating other tools into our collaboration platform became necessary, which is something we're able to do on Slack. One feature we're now exploring is the ability to invite key vendors and important customers into our projects. This allows us to share and collaborate with them, as well as our entire team.

## Communication & Collaboration: Video-Based Tools

Once you have replaced email communication, you'll need to replace your in-person meetings. Video requires 100 percent engagement and presence. It's the closest you'll get to face-to-face in a virtual workspace. When we started working remotely, I required video calls for all team interactions. I didn't want them picking up their phones to discuss work-related issues because I needed them to be efficient and focused on their conversations.

I will tell you, it wasn't easy—and still, after many years, there are those who try to avoid it. Many want to hide behind their phone and will say they don't want to be seen on camera. You'll hear things like, "I don't have makeup on," or, "I look like crap today." The reality is, it takes more effort to be on video.

Here's the truth: No one can multitask and say they are fully engaged. It isn't humanly possible. In a face-to-face conversation, you must give your full attention to the other person. You can't shop online, check text messages, or scroll through your social media feed. Not only is it considered rude, but it is also impossible to fully pay attention to either task (the conversation or your phone). You will inevitably miss details. Phone calls allow people to wander, drift, and not be completely engaged or present in the conversation. Video is the closest thing to an in-person conversation as you'll get in a virtual setting.

This is why video remains fundamental and foundational in our team building efforts and our effectiveness; it's necessary.

Plus, there are additional side benefits of using video:

- The ability to share screens, review documents as a team, demonstrate websites, etc. without the need for a projector and/or special setup.
- The ability to record video meetings (group or one on one). A recording of the video meeting can be a valuable asset. Team members can access a recording if they're unable to make a meeting. It can also serve as documentation for HR during disciplinary meetings and performance reviews.

If you do record video interactions, be upfront about it. I also suggest you include a disclaimer about the use of recordings in your remote work agreement.

Be aware that behavior often changes when people know the call/video is being recorded. One of the complaints for video will be that someone must get out of their pajamas, comb their hair, or take a shower. Yes, you do expect employees to be presentable, showered, and dressed appropriately when they work from home. If you were to do a quick google search, you'd see articles on "how to be productive at home" say that being showered and dressed appropriately is always at the top of the list. So, yes, there is a reason, and I don't feel it's too high of an expectation. We're not asking for suits and ties, but a clean, groomed, neatly dressed appearance is a requirement.

And while video remains a necessary component for enhanced efficiency of a virtual team, don't expect to see results from the start. Getting used to these new ways will take some time. Ease into it by assembling a small team for a planned video meeting. At first, you might notice the team is distracted by all the novelty. They're trying to figure out their role: when (and how) to raise their hand, unsure of when to jump in, etc. Body language is different on video as well. People are often uncomfortable. Their eyes may wander. They may fidget or constantly seem to be reaching for something. Such behaviors are actually quite normal.

It drove me crazy at first as I read the body language of everybody and watched them looking around at everyone else, looking at how they looked on camera. It does level out... eventually. The newness wears off after a month or so and then you can get down to business.

Difficult as it might be to remain patient as everyone learns the new way of doing things, it's critically important that you and your team master video. Meetings need to be of quality and substance (we'll expand on this later). While things started out a little rough for our company, today, our video chats are often more effective than the previous in-person office meetings. It's become such a useful tool that we now require our key vendors/partners to use video when meeting with our team members. We need everyone to embrace our culture to achieve maximum performance and connectivity.

As far as platform is concerned, video may be a feature that's offered in your text-based tool (like it was when we used Glip). Or you may decide to utilize a separate video tool for your company's needs. Many excellent tools currently exist (Zoom, Google Meet, Microsoft Teams, etc.), and you've most likely experienced one or more yourself. We started out by utilizing the video feature that was included with our phone service package from RingCentral, which is powered by Zoom video. We use this for all of our one-on-one client and vendor meetings and internal team conferences.

## Phone System

For about half of my team, quality phone service isn't a luxury, but a necessity. They spend about 60 percent of their day on the phone coaching clients. The customer pays a lot for each of these meetings, so their expectations of quality are high as well. Each call lasts anywhere from 30 minutes to two hours. These calls are my team's bread and butter—quite literally. In the office, they had access to a high-quality IP/internet phone system. Unfortunately, it was designed for a brick-and-mortar building and couldn't go with us when we transitioned into the remote office.

After extensive testing of different systems, we chose RingCentral as our provider. I loved the idea of a "soft-phone" (using a computer to make and receive calls). The idea of having a large office phone on my desk at home felt like old thinking (and, at the most, a transition piece of hardware).

Regardless of which vendor you choose, it's imperative to document all of your current extensions, voicemails, greetings, etc. as you currently have them in the system. (This proved to be a rather tedious step for our company.) Also, be sure to factor in the time it'll take to port numbers from your current carrier to your new one, assuming a change is necessary.

When it was all said and done, our cost per workstation (including long distance service and all other fees) came to $75 each per month. This cost is comparable to that of our old phone system, but we also have the additional benefit of video meetings and the included collaboration tools. RingCentral has also been more reliable than our brick-and-mortar phone solution. Since switching over seven years ago, we've experienced about 10 minutes of downtime—total.

I feel like we're getting greater value with our remote service. I also firmly believe that IP phones are the only way to go in a remote work environment. Going this route increases the bandwidth needed by each employee, especially if they'll be using video, but the reliability and value are worth it. If phone service is even half as critical in your business as it is in ours, I suggest you have a backup IP phone system already in place. We use Skype, which costs us about $8 a month, per employee. Of course, I would strongly urge against having your individual employees use their own devices for company matters. A similar option would be to provide each employee with their own company-issued mobile device (which some companies already do), but again, there are many other options that can provide benefits above and beyond a standard mobile device.

## Software & Applications

Our company was always a Microsoft shop. For a smooth transition, I elected to stay with Windows and Office but initially moved everything to Office 365, Microsoft's Cloud package. We've since transitioned to using Google Workspace.

To help you determine the best fit for your team, there are a few key software features you should keep in mind. First, most software programs today are internet based, or moving there quickly. When available, I prefer using software with a desktop connection since the web-based programs can be a bit clunky. That being said, it's important to note that the internet and desktop versions are connected, so nothing is saved on our desktops. Everything's feeding back through the web, and it's an improved interface than the desktop-only version. At the time of printing, many of the desktop versions are being phased out, and the providers are moving to 100 percent internet based. (I guess they were working out the kinks too!) It seems to be working okay thus far.

Another key component of necessary software programs for your virtual team may be the ability to access the program on a mobile device. Team members may need to stay connected while away from their home office, and mobile applications can fill that gap. As time goes on and work becomes more integrated with mobile devices, these applications will become increasingly necessary for your employees. This is especially true for your key players.

As a leader, I'm constantly interacting with my team—checking in while sitting in the waiting room at my doctor's office, stopping for gas, traveling for work, or grabbing a bite to eat. Applications give me the mobile accessibility I need to keep projects moving forward, regardless of where I am or what I am doing.

It would be wonderful if all of the programs used by your team were internet-based and accessible by mobile device. It's also highly unlikely. Take inventory of the internal programs used in various departments, such as your accounting system, custom CRM, and/or internal knowledge base. You'll need to assess each one with your IT person, and start asking questions about options for when you go virtual.

My biggest concern was whether some of our legacy systems could be moved out of the office server environment. We were able to successfully move Great Plains, Microsoft's monster accounting system, onto a remote server. It was a difficult and expensive task, but once the transition was complete, I knew it would be possible for any online system.

The transition may require you to seek help from an outside vendor that specializes in a particular software. Be sure you stress that the company will no longer have a physical location when talking with them. Since most software is moving off the desktop and into internet-based versions, odds are that they'll be able to find a solution that fits your needs. It might be a bit clunky at first, but you can almost bet there will be an upgraded version soon.

## File Sharing and Storage

One thing to work on before going virtual is to break everyone from the habit of saving files to their desktop and/or laptop hard drive. This is necessary not only for document sharing purposes when your company is full-time virtual, but it's also the most effective way to safely store files. I cannot stress this enough: it is not a smart business move to rely on backups to recover lost work that was saved on a hard drive. Backups rarely suffice. Backing up everyone's system (and their docs) was a nightmare for our IT guy. I can't count how many times a CEO has lost a super important report or file because their hard drive failed—after all, it isn't "if" a hard drive fails, but "when." (And usually, it's the CEO who loses the most important items, so start your training from the top down). Everyone needs to be in the habit of storing files in the cloud and sharing them on the ONE interface the company has selected for document storage. (For example, you don't want some employees using OneDrive and some using Google Drive; they all must be on the same platform.)

You can handle sharing and storage in many ways. Documents that aren't accessed regularly can be saved in a less expensive place. Important and more frequently used items should be saved somewhere accessible and easy to use. (I suggest getting help from your IT person when making your decisions.)

At the time I conducted my research, Dropbox was the most expensive. Google Drive and Amazon were the least expensive, and there were several other solutions in between. While I liked the functionality and usability of Dropbox, it was too pricey for us (it might be more feasible for smaller teams who need less storage). If you have Office 365 or Windows 10 and plan to continue using these options, OneDrive is included with that software package and is an option to explore for your document sharing and storage needs. Although we tested this platform, it didn't quite suit our needs.

We ultimately decided to go with Amazon S3 to store most of our "rarely accessed" files. We went with Glip, our collaboration tool, to share and store the more frequently accessed files and eventually transitioned to Google Drive.

Amazon has a ton of storage options, including one where you're only charged when a file or resource is accessed by you or someone on your team. This is the option we went with. I rarely ever see a bill for Amazon; the cost doesn't meet the threshold for needing my approval.

Glip allowed us to upload frequently used files into individual, team, or project "rooms." This allowed them to be shared, accessed, and edited by other team members. We used the note feature to keep these files from getting lost in the trail of chat messages. Google Drive allows you to grant access to certain folders as needed. For instance, we have an HR-shared HR drive where only I and the HR person have access to it.

Afraid it'll be too difficult to get your entire team on the same page? IT can map favorites and make other adjustments to help minimize confusion and ease the transition. I stressed the importance of proper sharing and storage by telling my team that I should be able to grab their laptop at any time and switch it with a new one without them losing a single item. That threat alone made them think and work harder to properly preserve their files.

Don't feel required to implement a fancy file sharing system. You could have the most intricate cloud system in the world, but if employees can't quickly access what they need, they'll ask someone to send it to them (likely via email). People want things to be easy. A good collaboration tool will include some form of file sharing, as well as a good search function to easily find things deemed as "somewhere."

No matter where you store your files, you'll need a basic organization system. I categorize "files" in three ways:

- **Personal Files**: These are the files an employee uses for their job. They may not be shared, but they are accessed periodically. In the past, these files might have been stored under "My Documents" on a person's hard drive. Our policy now is that nothing is saved on a desktop or local system. Everything is mapped to save into the cloud-based drive. It took a while for everyone to get in the habit of saving their docs to the cloud, but once we said, "we're not backing this up anymore," everyone's behavior changed.

- **Working Files**: These are any files shared by two or more employees. The creator of the file shares the file so that others can contribute, read, edit, etc. This works really well for content creation projects, as it normally involves a lot of people to add to a website, blog, etc. We started using OneDrive for this but are now using Google Drive. The team, as a whole, is still getting used to sharing documents, but the heavy users are loving it. The shared links to these files are often in the team's Slack room, so they're easily found and accessed. (Docs related to open enrollment, vacation schedules, etc. are uploaded to the "Bulletin Board" room we have created in Slack. The employees now know where to go, and these periodically needed docs don't have to be emailed around when someone needs them. Our HR manager keeps these files current.)

- **Dead/Archive Files**: These are files that would only need to be accessed for an audit or some other abnormal event. Every archived file in our company is kept in an Amazon S3 account. I consider this "dead storage," but it's still necessary. Keeping it in a storage system separate from our main file storage system saves the company valuable space for important, pertinent documents.

# CHAPTER 3

# THE NEW WORKING SPACE

You will know when your employees are "settled" into their new remote environment. They're not distracted by all of the things that happen at home, and perhaps they'll have developed a deeper relationship with their dog. They have started to form new social connections to replace the old habits (Zoom lunches with coworkers, virtual happy hours, breakroom chats, etc.). Video meetings aren't distracting anymore, and you're able to get right down to business. You might have a few rebels still calling each other on the phone, but the vast majority of the team understands that video improves the quality of each interaction. Your team will report—and your KPIs will show—that more work is getting done. The technology kinks will be worked out, leaving everything running smoothly. Your IT and HR departments will know how to support everyone in this new environment.

To ensure you get to this place, this chapter will cover what to be prepared for when you transition to your new virtual working space.

## The Home Office

While being able to work at home is a great benefit that must be factored and leveraged appropriately, it's not a perk just for the employees. Your company stands to save a lot of cost by moving its workforce remote. Employees know this too. You'll quickly see a line must be drawn in regard to what the company will pay for and what it won't. This is especially true when it comes to the employees' home office space.

Your shift to a remote environment may feel as though you're essentially "forcing" your employees to either get on board and work from home or find a new, non-remote job. Does this automatically make it the company's responsibility to ensure that each employee has an ideal workspace? As an example, consider the employee who lives in a small studio apartment with their very large dog. You need them to have a quiet space to work, and the dog could be an issue, especially if a delivery is made or there's a lot of activity outside that will encourage the dog to bark. Will the company supplement the rent of this employee to ensure they can afford a larger, quieter workspace?

Another example is utilities. Is the company going to compensate their employees for the inevitable increase in electricity costs that are bound to occur when they start working from home? What about the expenses of high-speed internet for those who currently don't have internet or only carry a basic package? How about the perks and benefits that employees will automatically lose once they're no longer working at the office (i.e., having to pay for their own coffee, creamer, sugar, paper towels, etc.)? These are real questions that *will* come up as you discuss the remote environment.

I encourage you to be prepared and consider how the company might keep things "fair" across the board and support your employees in setting up an environment conducive to their—and the company's—overall success in the remote world. Remember that being respectful of your team's concerns is a major part of this transition. There are no bad ideas. Help them feel heard by taking each question in, evaluating the potential solutions, and deciding on a solution that's best for everyone. I also recommend starting light on your commitment. It's easier to add perks than try to take them away once they're given.

By Referral Only allowed employees to transfer certain things from their physical office space to their remote one, such as their office chair and computer stations. This didn't add any cost for us, and it was an immediate benefit for employees. We chose to also provide a hard phone with softphone capability, a headset, and a webcam for the internal video meetings. Most everything else we deemed the responsibility of individual employees.

Many appreciated being able to purchase their own desk; they could find one that fit their space and personal preferences. Several purchased a stand-up unit that can raise and lower the workspace, allowing them to either sit or stand while working, which studies say is beneficial for individual health. The company now purchases stand-up desk add-ons at the employee's request. It's a nice perk and not too expensive. (If the employee wants something fancy, you could offer to contribute the cost of basic and then send them out shopping on their own dime for the extra bells and whistles.)

After these decisions were made, there wasn't much left to consider. Few employees actually need a printer for their home office. In fact, if you really look at what people are printing, it's usually personal items. The same with a copier. There are exceptions, of course. Your accounting department will likely need a multifunction printer with scanner and fax. The marketing department may need a color printer. Your company may decide to provide these, as necessary.

Most of our employees had some sort of internet connection for their personal life. We required an upgraded internet bandwidth to run our phone lines and video meetings. I thought it would be fair to subsidize each employee the same amount. We rounded up to $50 per employee as a reimbursement on their paycheck. This covered the upgrade in the cases of an employee who had the basic service, but it still kept it fair for those who already had high-speed.

Most companies provide office supplies, even after going virtual. Our managers use one Amazon account to purchase supplies for their entire team. Items are then disbursed, based on need, which is actually quite minimal. Perhaps it's because the appeal of hoarding supplies is gone, or maybe it's just that people waste less when they work from home. Either way, when you clean out the supply closet and send everyone home with a stash, you're likely to find enough supplies to last a while (a good five years or more). Start by distributing these items first, then come up with a plan on how you'll order new supplies as they run out.

Most of our team felt privileged to work from home. They were genuinely excited to set up their new space, and we didn't hear a lot of grumbling. Perhaps we were just generous enough. When it comes to your company's transition, remember that you can be as accommodating as you like, but you have to be consistent. Your HR department should be able to help with this.

I also recommend having your IT person install all the computers, review the internet setup, test the bandwidth, and review the set-up of each home office space in person. My guy reported back with a detailed overview, thus serving as my eyes and ears so I knew who needed more support.

## Employee Workstation

Originally, I assumed we'd simply send the office desktop units home with our employees. It made sense at the time; we owned the machines, and they worked just fine. I didn't see a point in adding more cost to our transition. Unfortunately, I learned (the hard way) that a desktop isn't an optimal setup for a home office. If anything, desktop units in the home office hinder performance and productivity.

Remember how I said a fire, flood, or power outage shouldn't disrupt the flow of your business? Well, in that first year of working remotely, our employees faced numerous challenges in their home offices—issues that wouldn't have been issues if we'd traded out our computer systems to swap the desktops for laptops in the very beginning.

As obvious as it sounds, the problem is that a desktop is not portable, so any reason that made it difficult for an employee to work in the exact spot where the desktop was set up would interrupt business. For example, an employee would have family members visit from out of town. Suddenly, they had a bunch of small children running around the home, creating noise, and distracting them from their work. A termite infestation could leave an employee incapable of working for days, perhaps even weeks. Home remodels, flooding, and other common events were problems because the employee simply couldn't do the work from home—not without noise, distraction, and a loss in productivity.

We realized our employees needed the ability to unplug their units and find somewhere more suitable to work, should their home be invaded or otherwise compromised. (We'll discuss what a suitable "somewhere" looks like shortly.) The optimal setup for our company ended up being a laptop that connects into a docking station, which provides the employee with a standard monitor/keyboard/ mouse experience. These features are offered, regardless of where our employees are working for the day. Within five minutes of plugging into the internet or Wi-Fi, they can start working from any location without sacrificing productivity. I had to use one to "get it" and believe in it. Now it's the only way I work.

You might be interested to learn that the ability to escape distractions and challenges at the home office isn't the only benefit to using a laptop and docking system. Another unintended (but highly coveted) perk is the ability for managers to take longer vacations. Instead of rushing back home to conduct a meeting, they can conduct a virtual one from where they're vacationing. They can even do short, simple projects in between all the fun. Their equipment goes with them, after all. The same benefit would be available to your employees as well. For my key leaders carrying heavy workloads, we have a "true up" system for when they're on vacation. Oftentimes, they'll need to do certain work during their vacation. They don't always know how much time it will take, so when they return, they may reduce the time submitted for their vacation (sometimes by as much as a day or two) if they spent more time working on vacation than anticipated.

Now, maybe you're thinking like I did in the beginning—that a laptop setup is just too expensive. True, there are some initial costs to consider, but the overall financial burden is typically on par with desktop systems. Our company uses the Lenovo ThinkPad. These high-quality machines cost about $1,200 to $1,500, but they can be plugged into a docking station (approximate cost is $250) that lights up the monitor(s) and connects a keyboard, mouse, webcam, and headset. All of these items work the same on a laptop as they do on a desktop. (See Appendix C for the exact equipment I chose to outfit our teams with.)

This isn't an overnight process. You may only have the budget to purchase a few units at a time. (It took us a year to replace all of our desktops with the laptop docking system.) The point is to start planning for the future now. Know what you are working toward and use that vision to propel your company toward its goals in upcoming decisions. For example, if a desktop computer goes out tomorrow and you plan to transition the entire company to a laptop system over the next 12 to 18 months, fiscally (and logically) speaking, it makes more sense to upgrade the unit now.

Other safe purchases include a basic webcam and headset (about $100 for both). These have USB plugs that will work on your current setup and at the home office. They're also necessary for implementing the first step: helping your team feel comfortable with virtual meetings. Regardless of when (and how) you plan to migrate from the office, providing these basic tools and familiarizing your team with them allows your team to mentally prepare for the coming changes. The sooner you get started, the smoother their transition to the home office is likely to be.

## Collaborative & Temporary Workspace

While in your physical location, you may have frequently or regularly met for team meetings or other events. Perhaps many of your team members work directly with each other day to day. Chances are, there's a lot of collaboration happening. Prior to transitioning to virtual work, you'll need to consider whether your company will need some type of collaborative or temporary physical workspace. Not every business needs a permanent collaborative space, but I believe there is a need for a temporary place for employees to work—even if its sole purpose is to serve as a transition space.

There are situations in which employees might need a collaborative space later down the road. Reasons can range from that out-of-town family member and their four kids to remodeling projects. You'll want employees to have a quiet, private space to work. My team spends most of their day on the phone. They need a calm and quiet environment to be productive. Starbucks simply doesn't cut it, especially for my high producers. (In my opinion, it's too loud and distracting of an environment anyways.)

So, really, our decision to have "some space" available for our team, should they need it, helped to ease their minds during the transition. They knew they could still work "from home," even if home got in the way. Plus, they were already used to being in an office, so working out of a different location wouldn't be an abrupt change for them.

We considered two options: having a dedicated space that held four or five desks and some office equipment or using a shared (collaborative) workspace, sometimes called a coworking space. Collaborative workspaces are designed as a group of offices that are owned, rented out, and managed by a third-party company. You'll often see executives, entrepreneurs, accountants, tax professionals, and insurance brokers using these offices—a lot of one-person operations. The rooms can be reserved for your company's use daily, weekly, monthly, or as needed.

For our company, we determined that the dedicated space would have made more sense if there was going to be a lot of usage, but my gut said it wouldn't be used as much as many suggested. We decided to go with the shared workspace. At the time, it was a bit of a coin flip, but in the end, we found we chose correctly!

Ultimately, setting up another office space with internet, phones, and office equipment went against our philosophy of embracing our new identity as a remote company, and the shared space suited our needs perfectly. We particularly liked the executive quality furnishings, receptionist, and "big company" feel of the collaborative space. (It's also great if you plan to continue meeting with clients face to face.)

Cost was also a factor. The minimum fee for a dedicated office was around $1,500 per month. Our shared space is less than $300. Our plan allocates a certain number of hours of office use per month. If we use more than that, we pay for it. I encouraged employees to use it as much as they wanted during the initial test—no limits. This helped me determine how much they were hanging onto their old ways.

We've only gone over our maximum hours a couple of times—typically, it's been when we had a lot of in-person meetings. Employees will often decide to continue working in the shared office space on those days. It saves them from having to commute home in the middle of the work day. We don't mind paying for the extra, especially since it's so rare, and it increases their productivity.

Just be sure to clearly define with your team what the intention of the space is. It's not for the three employees who refuse to work from home and want to sit in the office every day to stay together and prove a point. You'll have to deal with those employees directly.

Besides our monthly hour-based plan, we book extra offices and meeting rooms during our quarterly meetings since we have people flying in from out of town. During these meetings, we spend our time connecting with our employees and teams (more on the importance of this later).

We've also seen several side benefits to the shared office space. We have access to meeting rooms, as large or small as needed. Plans vary, but with ours, only the (very large) executive conference room requires an additional fee. We honestly didn't feel we had a need for it. It also gives us an official mailing address, a central location for all of our mail. The coworking management company's receptionist sorts and holds it for us.

If your employees are spread out to some degree already, you may need to be creative in finding places they can go when they can't work at home. A lot of this depends on the job they're doing. One of our challenges is that my team is on the phone coaching clients most of the day. Sitting in a coffee shop, library, or a busier "communal" style coworking space doesn't work. In all honesty, I don't believe it works for most jobs. It's just too distracting. You're not able to completely focus on your work. It's fine if you're traveling or on vacation, or you're just "checking in," but to really work a full day and be productive, it's not the place.

Utilizing a coworking space will help ease the transition for your employees. They're good at making it easy. You don't have to bother shopping for it more than 60 days in advance, however. They're ready for you to move in and start using an office tomorrow. I'd say to put it on your to-do list during the last 30 days before you move. Regus and Pacific Workplaces are both examples of nationwide spaces with facilities available to use in any part of the country. There should be a handful of local ones to include in your search as well.

# CHAPTER 4

# MANAGING A REMOTE TEAM

No one wants to admit it, but working from home can be difficult. Distractions abound. From the house cleaning and personal phone calls to the FedEx guy and random visitors, there are always things vying for your attention. Sometimes you can check in and be responsive, yet still get nothing done. There's no room for days like this in the full-time virtual office. As a manager, I looked at it as a perk to work from home when the plumber was coming or my kid was sick. Now, it is simply how we function as a company. The key to eliminating unproductive days is preparation. Your role as a manager is to assume nobody is completely ready to work from home all of the time and act accordingly.

# Management by KPI

As mentioned in an earlier chapter, one technique for determining the productivity of your remotely working team is to monitor your key performance indicators (KPIs). Before the transition, take a look at your KPIs to determine (or at least understand) which ones will be available when you make the transition. In some cases, you may need to rebuild KPIs from (or into) your new software/hardware. Others may require you to come up with a whole new way to measure productivity.

For example, if you are dealing with a call center, KPIs like total daily talk time, average talk time per call, and number of calls per hour will probably be important data points to track as you move into the remote work area. Collecting data both "before the move" and "after the move" will allow you to compare the two.

In a department like accounting, you can often manage through business promises and commitments. An example might be that accounting has to enter all payables into the system within 24 hours of receipt, or the customer service department needs to clear and respond to inquiries within 24 hours. You might also require your employees to inform you of when (and why) these rules or commitments are broken. (I prefer to manage this way.)

# Establish Hours

I think there is a six month "novelty" period for someone who's working remotely for the first time. During this time, they learn how to stay focused while at home and how to balance the personal items that come their way during the workday. It's still amazing to me that others view me as "available for anything at any time" because I work from home. Yes, there's flexibility, but the work has to get done! As a manager, supporting your team through this novelty period should involve establishing and committing to regular work hours.

Some employees think being remote means working at any time of the day or night. Freelancers and entrepreneurs often do this, which allows them to balance multiple clients, along with their personal lives. Your employees need to understand that there is a difference.

When we first transitioned, I told everyone that we'd give this a try and if it failed, we'd all go back to the office. Interestingly, I had a few people who were really trying to prove that "this works." They would work at night, after hours, trying to be uber-productive to show that they could be successful with remote working. It was a benefit they wanted to hang onto, and they were so committed to it working that we were more productive than ever that first year.

And of course, productivity is great! But, I had adjustments to make, because business happens during the day, not after hours. Collaboration, camaraderie, and team support happen during traditional working hours. Allowing employees to make their own schedule is going to disrupt the flow. As a manager, you need to know when they're working on their projects and when they're interacting with their peers and customers. Setting regular business hours will help with this.

After our transition, we changed our shifts slightly since employees didn't have to commute anymore, but for the most part, we kept shift times the same. We generally set regular hours between 7 a.m. and 6 p.m., depending on where the employee lives. We have people located from coast to coast, so we try to have people working during those regular hours for their time zone. Another thing to keep in mind is whether you are managing a salary team versus a commission-based team versus an hourly team. Things may need to shift depending on their status.

Again, remember that the goal is to try to mimic what is most productive in your current workforce. It's typically best to avoid changing too many things during a major event, such as going remote. You can always lighten up, but it's hard to clamp down after things go awry.

Depending on your culture, you may want to install software that tracks your employee's "active" time on their computer. Banks and health care companies often use this. Time Doctor, Roadmap App, and Tickspot are a few popular time trackers on the market.

You'll likely see a shift in behavior with employees around their lunch times and break times. They probably won't be heading out to lunch with their department as often or running errands during lunch. Instead, they'll be making something quick in their kitchen because it's easy, convenient, and healthier. They will also like the money they're saving by not going out to eat.

We also noticed an unexpected positive during our transition: increased happiness among our employees. Almost every video call I'm on has a dog in the background, happily hanging out with its owner. We encourage our pet-owning employees to walk their dogs at lunch and play fetch on their breaks. It boosts morale... for everyone, even the pets!

It's also okay to allow your employees the freedom and flexibility to have the plumber drop by while they're working (versus having to take a half day off from the office). I would suggest that you discourage people from doing chores and errands (laundry, cleaning, etc.) during the work day, however. These tasks are often time intensive and distracting. You need them focused and engaged during working hours.

## The Importance of Video

As discussed earlier, video is a critical component of the virtual workspace. In fact, every meeting you have with your employees—whether individually or with a team—should be on video. Some employees will not be comfortable with video. It is typically the same people who don't like having their picture taken. Regardless of their reason for being camera shy, these employees are going to have to get over their issues, one way or another.

Video will be one of your greatest tools as a manager, for many reasons. In addition to what we discussed earlier—that employees are less distracted and more engaged on video versus phone—the ability to watch body language is another reason to enforce calls through video. As a manager, pay attention to this unspoken form of communication, especially when in meetings. Are people receptive to what you're saying? Are they buying in? Are they fully understanding and comprehending? Facial expressions, eye contact, and other forms of body language can be assessed on video. With a phone call, email, or chat, someone could be flipping you off or rolling their eyes at you, and you'd never know.

The last reason for using video goes back to your employee's workspace. During this transition, and the years that follow, being connected to your employees is imperative. You need to see the environment your employees are in at home. This is what your customers may be hearing or seeing! Examples can range from loud music, pets, or screaming children in the background to frequent interruptions and distracted behaviors (i.e., looking toward the door or at something in the room, rustling papers, etc.).

It might feel like you're being overly invasive, but you need to know if someone has a two-year-old in the home or a husband who is home all day and seems to have a desire to pop in and check on things a bit too frequently. Or, for example, if someone has their mother-in-law living with them and they're responsible for her care, the manager needs to know. Whether the employee realizes it or not, these are all potential distractions that can impact their productivity and focus during the work day, which, in the end, makes it your business to know.

I recommend that managers hold one video conference per month with each person on their team. It can be a check-in call of 30 minutes—it doesn't have to be long. The call can be all personal, or you could discuss how the person feels about their new virtual role, etc. It just needs to be an open forum where you are looking in their eyes and listening to what they have to say, while noticing their environment. There is no other way for you to determine whether this is working for them, whether they've "got it." You have to connect with them consistently.

No matter the level of employee, everyone gets at least 30 minutes from me every month. I meet with my key managers (at least) once a week for an hour. Team meetings occur at least once a month for one hour. There may be more communication among certain team members, depending on what projects might be going on at the time, but they typically keep things moving forward on their own. All managers meet with their people one on one, consistently. I try to be the example. As you and your team transition to the virtual office, I highly encourage you to do the same. Make the time for your own meetings. You (and your team) will enjoy the connection, and you'll learn a lot if you're paying attention.

## Face-to-Face Connection

Face-to-face meetings are still the best way to communicate and connect with your team, and with each individual. However, connecting face to face can be more challenging in the remote work environment.

If you are transitioning from everyone being together to working remotely, it will be easier to get everyone together for weekly or monthly face-to-face meetings as most of your employees will still be local. What you do in the first year will likely be different than the subsequent ones, however. Local employees will move out of the area, and you'll (hopefully) start to hire talent outside of your area. At this point, you'll have to get more creative when it comes to scheduling in-person meetings with your teams.

How often your company conducts in-person meetings will likely depend on budget and the situation. A good place to end up is for the entire team to meet in person at least four times per year. (Possibly a bonus holiday party would be appropriate for your culture.) Of course, if everyone is spread out all over the country (or the world), bringing everyone together quarterly might be too cost prohibitive. In this case, a yearly retreat/get-together should be added to the budget.

Team members who've never met face to face need this in-person connection to improve group cohesiveness. It is equally important for those who are used to seeing their colleagues every day. In our first year of being separated, I flew in for face-to-face meetings every six weeks. My employees wanted a higher frequency. They'd grown accustomed to seeing me at the office each day. Having me "disappear" after we went virtual and I moved out of state was difficult for them at first, but they slowly adjusted.

Our first meetings were interesting. The first 20 minutes were dominated by chit-chat. As tempting as it was to try to stifle this, I knew better. My team needed that time, so I started to plan for it. Today, I pad every meeting by 30 minutes. I also attempt to have at least one lunch, breakfast, or walk with my key team members. I'm not able to do it every quarter, but I make it a priority. My number one job is to maximize the time we have together. (On that note, I highly suggest you avoid working when doing in-person meetings with your team. Keep team activities and social-type interactions your priority for that time.)

You might have a few team members who try to wiggle out of these meetings, saying they're too busy or have other commitments. I highly recommend against letting this happen. If they can't plan to be away from work, with the team, for two hours a few times a year, you have bigger problems. (Be aware that the sooner you can get things on the calendar, the better it will be for the team.)

Be committed to having some face-to-face interactions with all of your team members. It matters. Be creative with your scheduling. Maybe your company attends a trade show every year. If half the company is already committed to being there, it may make sense to extend it by a day or two and have other team members come out.

Meeting space isn't hard to find and shouldn't be super expensive. You may have already set up a coworking space, in which case you'll likely have access to a conference room and probably some smaller meeting rooms. If you choose to go completely virtual or don't have a coworking space, check with local hotels. They often rent rooms for the day. Don't be afraid to think outside the box. Get together at a nearby park or beach. Have a barbecue. We've even done after-meeting parties at one of the employees' homes. The company foots the bill for food and beverages. It's likely you have a few people on your team who love entertaining. Now's their chance!

Be sure you connect with your HR Department on how to handle travel expenses. Be upfront with your team on what you will cover and what you won't, right from the start. If they choose to relocate on their own, are you going to pay for them to travel back to your corporate meetings, or will they be responsible for the bulk of the cost? Are hotels covered? What about food, gas, and entertainment?

These are all things that need to be discussed and structure built around them. The last thing you want is to have an uncomfortable conversation with an employee about their $6,000 travel expense report when it should've been $1,500, but if you don't discuss things ahead of time, it's going to happen. It could be a situation where the company pays up to a certain amount or a percentage of the total expenses. Compensation may even depend on the employee's position in the company.

## Monitoring At-Home Habits

When employees are working from home, you'll need to be tuned into monitoring habits that you may have not seen in the office. One item to look for is dress code. While you may not have an official dress code you require your employees to follow, you probably don't want them showing up to meetings in their pajamas. Another issue that's bound to come up is children or other people in the home during work hours and the employees' desire to tend to their needs. Or you may have an employee who sets up their workstation in the heart of the home where people and animals roam freely throughout the day, or who wants to work from bed. What about naps? When they're home, the lure of their bed may be too strong for some employees to resist.

To solve for the bulk of these "at-home habits," we created a "distraction-free environment" policy. In fact, it's in every job ad we put out when looking to hire. This allows us to ensure all employees have distraction-free environments, whether that involves children, family members, a cat who loves to pop in and out of meetings, or an employee who decides to work in the kitchen or next to the front door. We don't require them to have a separate office, or to get rid of the cat, or send their family away for the day. Rather, the emphasis is on creating an environment that is free of distractions so they can work efficiently and effectively. As a manager, you'll need to be aware of when employees need support and further guidance with this.

Another challenge to prepare for is potential alcohol and drug use among your virtual employees while they're working at home. I'm not talking about an off-the-deep-end situation; it's unlikely that you have serious addicts on your payroll, as they are often detected (and subsequently terminated) fairly soon after hiring. Instead, I'm talking about people who have created a habit of cracking open a beer, a bottle of wine, or their favorite cocktail within five minutes of walking through the door after their long day at work. The "trigger" for them is being home, so what happens when they start working from home?

In some cases, it may be difficult for them to draw the line as clearly and decisively as before. Instead of a six o'clock cocktail hour, it may become five o'clock, four o'clock, or even three o'clock. Before you know it, they could be downing drinks over their lunch hour, only to continue for the rest of the day. Obviously, this is going to be very difficult to see when you're not in person. Having your eyes open, talking to team members regularly, and having varied meeting times can help you uncover potential problems.

Remember to be strong on requiring all meetings be via video and watch for clues. You may notice something subtle, such as the person drinking out of a tumbler and making a funny face. Maybe their eyes are bloodshot, or they're struggling to stay engaged in the conversation.

Perhaps their speech is slurred. They may make strange, irrelevant comments.

I know it sounds crazy, but these are the things you need to be tuned into as a manager of a remote team. Keep an eye on everybody during company functions. Do you notice someone going over-the-top wild? There might not be any immediate disciplinary action required, but pay attention. File the behavior in your HR memory bank. At some point down the road, you may need to piece together a situation and address it accordingly.

# CHAPTER 5

# THE NEW HUMAN RESOURCES

HR will have to make several adjustments once the company goes remote. Everything from payroll and health insurance to interviews and training will have to be done in a different way. The manner in which your HR department handles the challenges before them can greatly alter the success of your remote transition.

Prepare them early, provide them with the tools and training that they need, and do your best to help them see the benefits of their new role and things will be less chaotic.

# Getting HR Ready to Move

At the heart of every company, you have the HR department. Their main duty is to protect the interests, image, and success of their employer, but they're also responsible for the experience of the employees. They ensure each person has the resources, tools, and leadership necessary for achieving their highest potential. Preparing this department for the transition early on is the key to creating a smoother overall transition for the rest of your company.

One of the first obstacles will be to find new health care coverage for your employees. Most likely, your company's current plan is regional, so it will only cover the individuals who work and live in the area. Right now, your entire team may reside within the state, but it's unlikely to stay that way. In our first year of the remote transition, we had two employees relocate to another state. We also hired two individuals who lived in another state. Going remote will give your team the freedom to live wherever they want, and at some point, you may decide to expand your hiring pool to reach talent in other parts of the country (I highly encourage this!).

Regional plans will not cover your new (or relocated) out-of-state talent, so you'll need to find another option. The solution could be as simple as adding a PPO plan, or it could be as complicated as adding an entirely separate carrier. Work with your HR manager, and do your research to determine the best fit for your company moving forward.

We use our open enrollment period to refine and add health care plans as necessary. Some of this is a work in progress and takes time to smooth out. We've found that United Healthcare has PPO coverage in most states. So far, only my state, Idaho, is left out. I am on a local plan, with the company paying the same proportion as if I had the company plan. Employees in California are offered the HMO or PPO option, and the rest are offered just the PPO option.

Be aware that payroll will also become more complicated once you have employees in another state. You'll need to carry workman's compensation in their respective states. Our work comp policy covers us in every state except Ohio, where I have to obtain a separate policy. (This is an Ohio-specific situation). The cost is low, but it requires someone keeping up on it. There will also be individual state taxes for most but not all states, and unemployment insurance to pay in every state. Of all the states in which we have employees, only California has a disability requirement.

It's also important to know that if you're doing your payroll internally, things could get messy. Having employees in another state adds a great deal of complexity to your taxes and systems. Some states don't connect to payroll software automatically, so there may be some manual payments and reporting, depending on where your workers are.

Now might be the time to consider outsourcing for your payroll. External services such as Paychex, Netchex, or Quickbooks can make things easier to manage. Now that we are represented in a few large states, we've targeted our recruiting efforts to states where we already have employees. This makes the onboarding task much easier for HR!

## Hiring New Virtual Employees

As your company works toward its goal of moving 100 percent virtual, consider looking specifically for employees who have experience working remotely. It's likely you'll find them easier now, as the pandemic shutdowns forced many companies to go virtual. Thankfully, since the start of COVID, many now consider it a perk to work from home.[5] I highly encourage you to use this to your advantage.

Why is it so important to hire employees who already have working knowledge of virtual workspaces? The most obvious reason is that they are less likely to require hand holding as the company transitions to remote. They already have experience using some of the systems, processes, and applications found within remote workspaces, and they may even have some insights or morsels of wisdom that can only be gained through first-hand use. "Here's how I handle X situation and stay organized."

---

5 "Survey Reveals 76% of Global Office Workers Want to Continue Working from Home post-COVID-19" by Anita Kamouri, Ph.D. and Kate Lister, Global Workplace Analytics, June 2, 2020, https://globalworkplaceanalytics.com/brags/news-releases.

Having seasoned remote workers on your team can also help boost the overall team morale; they already see the benefit of going remote, so they're likely to be accepting and appreciative of the changes that are about to occur, which can encourage others on your team to more willingly accept the changes. In other words, gaining the trust, support, and appreciation of new employees and influencers within the workforce can go a long way in smoothing out the physical-to-remote transition.

As we worked toward going remote, I intentionally hired a couple employees who weren't local. I started them remotely, and we built our relationship that way. Today, they are some of my best team members. They helped test and validate many of the systems and technologies that we continue to use today.

Once you move remote, your interview practices will shift from in-person to virtual. This is something you may even consider implementing before the transition. Currently, I do all the hiring because I want to meet everybody we're considering. My process for hiring includes an initial interview over the phone, usually 15 to 20 minutes to determine if they are qualified. Our second interview happens on video. If the applicant can't figure out how to get a camera hooked up to their computer or doesn't seem to be fairly comfortable with it, it lends to the notion that remote technology may not be for them. (Not a tried and true fact, but something to keep your eye on.) Knowing this about a potential new hire before you transition may help you decide if they are able to quickly adapt to the new remote environment.

The video interview is also a good time for you to see what an applicant's office environment looks like. Are kids running around everywhere? Are they at a Starbucks? Pay attention to all the signs because this person will be working in that same environment if you hire them. In one interview I conducted, the woman was driving in her car while trying to talk to me on video. Let's just say she didn't work out. I'm glad I found out early in the process.

## Onboarding and Employee Training

New-hire onboarding and ongoing employee training are two additional areas that will need to shift within the HR world when your company goes virtual. HR will need to review your training for new hires and make modifications to the existing plan, incorporating your new virtual status. This may include going from paper documents to electronic documents, setting up employees for their benefits online, managing and activating login credentials for all the programs and software, and coordinating the ordering and setup of a new employee's work equipment.

HR can also help the new virtual employee to feel included as a company team member through providing them with videos that explain who we are, descriptions of each department, how we work together, etc. This way, new employees get an introduction to the organizational chart and the company as a whole, and they feel as though they are part of something larger than just a computer station at their home.

Your HR rep may then hand off the new employee to their manager for job-specific training. For both new employee onboarding and current employee training, we use Google Classroom. It allows us to walk employees through training modules on things like the new tools and software they'll be using on the job.

New employees may not balk at this, but current employees may need some extra encouragement. Our team used to do training in person, as a "class" or with department leaders. They may have teamed up with other employees to train on specific call techniques, etc. Now, we have Google Classroom training modules that provide recordings of those training calls. In fact, our training has vastly improved after our remote transition since everything is now organized and accessible to anyone at any time.

## Terminations and Layoffs

The first time you or your HR manager has to terminate an employee remotely might be extremely uncomfortable—for everyone involved. (Hopefully, you get a little time being remote under your belt and are comfortable on video before that happens.) But really, firing or laying off an employee is uncomfortable and awkward in person too. But the plus side of being remote is that it doesn't rattle the entire team like it did before, when someone was cleaning out their stuff or being escorted out. You can also control the messaging better.

Just make sure your IT department has their timing buttoned up so access to all systems is eliminated as soon as you start the call. In addition, your HR department must stay within the guidelines of final pay and complete all final paperwork based on state, industry, or company rules. Then they have to coordinate the retrieval of company equipment, which can be messy.

The cause for the termination will often influence your odds of getting the equipment back safely. If it's a layoff, you can tie the severance package to the safe return of your equipment, greatly reducing the risk of it being damaged or stolen. If you are firing a person, however, they may be more likely to lash out because of hurt or entitled feelings. For this reason, always keep terminations professional, just as you would in a physical space. Also, be prepared with a plan if you think there's a chance that an employee will retaliate. I once chose to send my IT guy with termination papers when he went to retrieve the equipment. Not ideal, but it worked!

Instead—or if you don't have a dedicated HR professional in-house—you could consider using a third-party company to assist. We currently use SDHR Consulting for our HR needs. They are the HR professionals and provide HR support and relevant legal advice. We pay by the hour when we need assistance. So, if we have a troubled employee, or someone's filed a complaint and we don't know what to do, we go to them. The benefit of using a third-party company like this is that they will have resources to support your company no matter what state your employees are located in. This eliminates the need to have your HR professional brush up on the laws of all 50 states!

# CHAPTER 6

# TRUST THE PROCESS

Congratulations! You just got a crash course in how to set up your company for successfully transitioning to work 100 percent virtually. The first five chapters gave you the nuts and bolts on how to do that, and I hope that information serves you well. But, at the end of the day, if you take only one thing from this book, please remember this: really, it's all about the culture. Virtual companies see success when the culture is right.

For us, it's been over six years since we went completely remote. The culture is set. It's stable. There will never be a return to the office. About half of our workforce has relocated across the United States. Why? Because they can. They are no longer restricted to staying in one area because they have a great job there. We hire only the best of the best, and we have very little turnover. Now when something happens that goes against the grain of our company culture, it sticks out like a sore thumb. Employees speak up or jump in to help, and the issues tend to self-regulate. As CEO, I rarely have to get involved because the culture is so obvious and so set that it's difficult to hide something that just doesn't work for us.

Culture is that intangible feeling you get when you're part of a team, and it's key in this transition process. Going virtual works with the right culture, and what is right for you may not look the same for anyone else. You just need to trust the process and trust that it will all play out to your company's virtual success.

And keep in mind that going virtual should never be merely a money-saving move for your company. You're not simply trying to purge your expense listing of all the in-person related costs. Going virtual is a different way of doing business that should operate as a benefit to both the company and the employees. My goal was to not lose a single employee during our transition, and we didn't.

Besides the culture, keep your eye on the technology. Tech changes constantly and you may not be able to ever find a one-size-fits all option. Jump in and see what works, and be open to shifting when something better comes around. We are always looking for the next best tool. You might notice someone on your team who loves to test out new software and apps. I encourage you to utilize them.

The bottom line is this: If you think remote is the right step for your company, don't wait. Take action now and keep your eye on the future!

# ABOUT THE AUTHOR

Jeff is in his 10th year with By Referral Only. He is CEO and a partner to Joe Stumpf. His unique ability is building teams that implement ideas, big and small, in an efficient way. Jeff has spent the last 25 years in operations, with expertise in logistics, customer service, and subscription service management, with the last six years executed with an effective, remote workforce. Jeff has managed software subscriptions as high as 50k shipments per month and owned his own children's software company. He will always lead a team.

# APPENDIX A

# TECH CATEGORIES

| Employee Workstation |
| --- |
| Computer |
| Phone |
| Desk |
| Chair |
| Printer |
|  |
| **Network/IT** |
| Physical Servers, Routers, Domain Controllers, etc. |
| Phone System |
|  |
| **Software** |
| Company CRM |
| Collaboration |
| Video Meetings |
| Telephone |
| Project Management |
| File Storage/Sharing |
| Email |
| Calendars |
| HR/Payroll |
| Warehouse/Order Management |
| Accounting System |
| Your Proprietary Business Software |
| Marketing Software |

# APPENDIX B

# SAMPLE SPREADSHEET FOR WAREHOUSE

| In-house Fulfillment Cost Example | | |
|---|---|---|
| Warehouse Labor (all-in) | $10,000 | (2 FTE's) |
| Warehouse Space Cost | $5,000 | (5K sq ft x $1/sq. ft) |
| Equipment Rental | $500 | (Forklift) |
| **Total Warehouse Costs** | **$15,500** | |
| | | |
| # of orders shipped | 1,000 | |
| # of line items/order | 2.5 | |
| | | |
| **Cost per order** | **$15.50** | (Total cost/total # orders) |

| 3rd Party Logistics Pricing Example | | |
|---|---|---|
| Pallet Storage Fee | $20 | 50 pallets used as example |
| Per Order Fee | $3 | (x number of orders) |
| Additional Line Item Fee | $1.75 | (x 1.5 additional line items/order) |
| | | |
| Total Pallet Storage Fee | $1,000 | ($20x50 pallets) |
| Total Per order Fee | $3,000 | ($3x1000 orders) |
| Total Add. Line Items Fee | $2,625 | ($1.75x1.5=2.625x1000 |
| **Total 3rd Party Costs** | **$6,625** | |
| **Cost per order** | **$6.60** | (Total cost/total # orders) |
| **Monthly Savings:** | **$8,875** | |

# APPENDIX C

# TECHNICAL STACK

Technology options are fast-moving targets! Here's my recommended hardware and software stack, as of the printing of this book.

**Home Office Setup:** (This has not changed much. Lenovo has been great.)

- 2 Monitors, Viewsonic 24" monitor ($190 on Amazon)
- 2 Monitor Stand/RIsers, 4" height ($26.95 on Amazon)
- 1 Lenovo ThinkPad Ultra Docking Station, 40AJ0135US ($220 on Amazon)
- 1 OEM Lenovo ThinkPad T490s Laptop 14" WQHD Display 2560x1440, Intel Quad Core i7-8565U, 8GB RAM, 256GB NVMe, Fingerprint, Win10P, ($1,359.95 on Amazon). We change these systems out every 3-4 years.
- 1 Logitech MK270 Wireless Keyboard and Mouse Combo
- 1 Logitech C922x HD Pro Webcam, Full HD 1080p ($94.90 on Amazon)
- 1 Headset, Plantronics Blackwire C3220 209745-201. This is the basic model. Your team will branch out and want to use different styles, wireless, etc. ($37 on Amazon)

**TOTAL: Under $2,000 for complete setup**

## Internet Bandwidth Minimum:

- 13mbps download, 2mbps upload. (Results vary depending on other home traffic, i.e., kids, movie streaming, and other business functions.)

## Workstation/Team Software:

- Slack (team collaboration and chat)
- Zoom (video webinars, meetings) Zoom's chat and phone are newer and appear to be stable.
- We are testing them now, with the plan to consolidate in the near future.
- RingCentral (phone and texting) They also feature Zoom white label video conferencing.
- Google Workspace (Gmail, Calendar, Doc Management, Drive, Suite)
- Zendesk (customer support/ticketing software)
- Amazon (public-facing document hosting)
- Wistia (public video hosting)
- Calendly (calendar scheduling system)
- Trello (project management)
- Infusionsoft (CRM)

www.ingramcontent.com/pod-product-compliance
Lightning Source LLC
Chambersburg PA
CBHW071924120726
48001CB00005B/1855